# THE EARLY HISTORY OF THE
# GAY RIGHTS
# MOVEMENT

# THE EARLY HISTORY OF THE
# GAY RIGHTS
# MOVEMENT

## GREG BALDINO

Rosen
YA

New York

*To Fen*

Published in 2019 by The Rosen Publishing Group, Inc.
29 East 21st Street, New York, NY 10010

**Library of Congress Cataloging-in-Publication Data**

Names: Baldino, Greg, author.
Title: The early history of the gay rights movement / Greg Baldino.
Description: New York : Rosen Publishing, 2019. | Series: The history of the LGBTQ+ rights movement | Includes bibliographical references and index. | Audience: Grades 7–12.
Identifiers: LCCN 2017019694 | ISBN 9781538381281 (library bound) | ISBN 9781508183082 (pbk.)
Subjects: LCSH: Gay liberation movement—History—Juvenile literature. | Gays—History—Juvenile literature. | Gay rights—History—Juvenile literature.
Classification: LCC HQ76.5 .B34 2018 | DDC 323.3/264—dc23
LC record available at https://lccn.loc.gov/2017019694

*Manufactured in the United States of America*

**On the cover:** A compilation of covers of *ONE* magazine, a pro–gay rights publication circulated in the 1950s and '60s (*top*), is shown here over a photograph of William Martin (*bottom left*) and Bernon Mitchell (*bottom center*), two US government agents who defected to the Soviet Union and were subsequently accused of being part of a traitorous homosexual spy network.

# CONTENTS

# INTRODUCTION

The LGBTQ+ community is diverse. It consists of a number of subgroups representing different gender and sexual minorities. The acronym "LGBTQ+" stands for "lesbian, gay, bisexual, transgender, and queer/questioning." The first three terms refer to sexual orientation, which is an individual's inclination in terms of sexual attraction to others. While heterosexual (or straight) people are attracted primarily to the opposite sex, those who are lesbian or gay are sexually attracted to the same sex. Those who are bisexual are generally attracted to both sexes.

Being transgender, in turn, relates to a person's gender identity, that is, their inner sense of gender. While a majority of people are cisgender, meaning they continue to identify with the gender their parents or doctor assigned them at birth, those who are transgender have a gender identity inconsistent with the one they were designated as a newborn.

Of course, those who are lesbian, gay, bisexual, or transgender are not the only gender and sexual minorities that exist. Therefore, many people add a "Q" and plus sign (+) to the acronym. The "Q" stands for "queer" or "questioning" and is meant to encompass people who may not fit neatly into one specific identity or may not yet know which identity best suits their sexual or gender identity. The plus sign accounts for other established gender and sexual minorities, including those who are intersex (those with genetic, hormonal, and physical features typically associated with both male and female), asexual (those who

In 1975, gay and lesbian organizations such as the National Gay Task Force marched to bring attention to a proposed Civil Rights Act amendment that would include gay people as a protected class.

do not feel sexual desire at all), pansexual (those whose sexual attraction is not limited by gender identity or sex), and nonbinary (those who do not associate with either a male or female gender identity).

While to some people it can seem like these communities formed out of nowhere, that isn't the case. Premodern LGBTQ+ history was a time of discreet liaisons and brutal rebuke. Historically, the LGBTQ+ community faced unforgiving intolerance and unjust persecution. But in an environment of discrimination and chastisement, early gay and lesbian rights organizations rose up to demand respect.

The time period of this movement's early history spans from the nineteenth century to the Stonewall riots of 1969. That is when the identities of LGBTQ+ people began to mold into those we recognize today. This period also documents how LGBTQ+ culture and communities were largely segregated between cisgender men, cisgender women, and those who were transgender until the latter half of the twentieth century. As LGBTQ+ identities have evolved, so, too, has the persecution of them, guiding the shape of the communities that formed in resistance.

The further back one goes, the harder it is to find evidence of LGBTQ+ history. The words we use to discuss gender and sexual minorities are relatively recently coined, so up until the last hundred years or so, people didn't have a common frame of reference for who they were. Also, the ostracism and discrimination that LGBTQ+ people have often faced caused many people throughout history to stay "in the closet," keeping their identity a secret. Historians have often omitted the sexual or gender identity of historical figures, and surviving family members have sometimes worked to hide the truth about LGBTQ+ people. While this resource strives to be as accurate as possible, it is in no way a complete portrait of the many LGBTQ+ people and communities that predate Stonewall.

# CHAPTER ONE

# THE DAYS OF PASSIONATE FRIENDSHIP

I n the 1800s, life for LGBTQ+ people in North America was quite different from life today. There were no publications about or organizations for the LGBTQ+ community, meaning its members had no resources for either the public or private spheres. There was not even a common language, as such terms as "homosexual," "transgender," and "bisexual" didn't yet exist. Attraction to someone of the same gender was not seen as a part of a person's identity or an involuntary expression or feeling, but rather a matter of free will.

Before the twentieth century, people generally lived at home until they were married. For somebody never to marry was somewhat unusual. As a result, it was difficult for LGBTQ+ people to have any kind of private life to explore their feelings and attractions. Many people would keep this part of their identity a secret for their entire lives and neglect their feelings for those they truly desired in order to adhere to society's norms.

This 1955 Bible study class is learning about Moses parting the Red Sea. People have historically been taught that homosexuality is wrong in churches, synagogues, mosques, and other houses of worship.

# FROM SCRIPTURE TO PRESCRIPTION

In many religious societies, homosexuality has been seen as a sin and treated as a theological and moral phenomenon that religious authorities policed. However, with the growth of secularism and the role of science in society following the eighteenth-century Enlightenment, a shift in cultural authority emerged.

Beginning in the early 1800s, doctors and medical researchers gained more and more authority as experts. Among the many changes that this brought about in the social landscape, there came a new understanding of homosexuality that shifted away from viewing it as an immoral choice freely chosen to an involuntary pathology that doctors thought could be cured.

In 1884, Dr. James Kiernan wrote in the *Detroit Lancet* about a twenty-two-year-old woman he had treated. The woman "liked to play boy's games and dress in male attire" and had admitted to feeling sexually attracted to her female friends. Kiernan attempted to cure her by prescribing cold baths and what he called "a course of intellectual training."

Nine years later, Dr. F. E. Daniel presented a paper at a medical conference titled "Should Insane Criminals or Sexual Perverts be Allowed to Procreate?" In his paper, he compared homosexuality to alcoholism and insanity, both of which he argued were hereditary. While he did say that "sexual perversity" should not be punishable by death, as some cultures believed, he did suggest

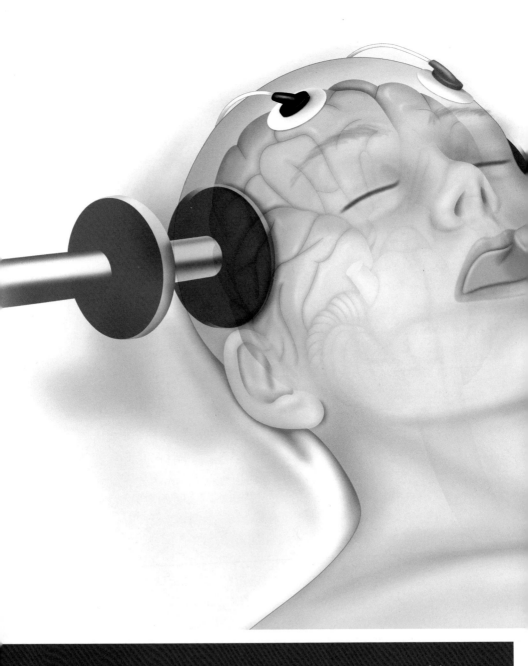

This illustration shows a person being put through electroconvulsive, or electroshock, therapy. Electroconvulsive therapy used to be a common form of conversion therapy, but it is now denounced as a form of abuse.

that homosexuals and the mentally ill should be medically prevented from having children so as not to pass on their conditions. As with other medical problems, doctors soon suggested "cures" for homosexuality. Surgery to remove the uterus, hormone injections, drug treatment, hypnosis, and electroshock therapy were some of the "treatments" used.

## NO THANKS, I'LL PASS

Some members of the LGBTQ+ community decided to try a new way to hide their identities. This approach, called passing, involves LGBTQ+ individuals attempting to hide their identities, typically by giving the false presentation of being heterosexual or cisgender. As early as the 1850s, gay men used immersion in bohemian culture as a method of passing. For women, whom society still expected to be defined by their relationships to men, adopting radical roles such as suffragettes and social reformers offered a form of cover—and, of course, there was always the nunnery.

During this time, life for women—regardless of their sexual identity—was very strictly regulated by social standards. Publicly, women could only engage in activities and behaviors that were considered appropriate for their gender, and they were economically dependent on men through marriage. While the Industrial Revolution and US expansion westward allowed men more freedom to find work and choose partners based on personal preference, women still had to marry based on their financial needs.

## FOR THE LOVE OF COMRADES

One of the most important figures in American LGBTQ+ history was the poet Walt Whitman. Born in 1819, he has been called the most influential American poet and the father of free verse poetry. Whitman's best-known work is the book *Leaves of Grass*, a collection of poems he self-published in 1855. The book was considered scandalous at the time for its vivid sensory

# NORTH AND SOUTH OF THE BORDERS

Like the United States, Canada and Mexico began as colonies of European powers. Canada was a colony of England, and Mexico was under the control of Spain.

At the start of the 1800s, Canada was an enemy of the recently independent United States. Mexico lost territory after the Mexican-American War (1846–1848.) This land was in the current states of California, Nevada, Texas, Utah, New Mexico, Arizona, and Colorado.

Canada did not achieve complete independence from Britan until 1982. Canada's laws about homosexuality were thus the same as England's. The first two men charged with sodomy, a term often used to refer to gay sex, were found guilty in 1841. Sex between men was punishable by death until 1869, although these sentences were commuted to imprisonment in Canada. In 1961, the penalty was changed to ten years of imprisonment. Persecution of homosexuals became stronger over the century, and the laws were worded in ways that gave local authorities almost complete freedom to press criminal charges.

(continued on the next page)

*(continued from the previous page)*

After winning its independence from Spain, Mexico was occupied by France, from 1862 until 1867. During this period, the new government adopted the system of law known as the Napoleonic Code, under which homosexuals were not considered guilty of a criminal offense. However, after the French lost power, Mexican states imposed laws against "attacks on morals and good customs," which were loosely worded so that gay men and lesbians, as well as other populations, could be charged with criminal behavior.

descriptions. But what was even more scandalous was his writings on the "love of comrades," which is how Whitman chose to talk about the love between two men.

For many years, Whitman was in a relationship with Peter Doyle, a streetcar driver he met in 1865, when the poet was in his forties. Doyle was more than twenty years younger, and Whitman was the only passenger that night. Doyle chose to strike up a conversation, even stopping the streetcar to talk with him. In his own words, Doyle said of their first meeting, "We were familiar at once—I put my hand on his knee—we understood." Whitman

This daguerreotype shows poet Walt Whitman posing for a portrait. This is thought to be the earliest surviving photo of him, although exactly when in the 1840s it was taken is uncertain.

rode the streetcar all the way to the end of the line and back that night, and the two were then inseparable until Whitman died of complications from pneumonia in 1892.

The circumstance of Whitman and Doyle's first meeting was how many gay men, lesbians, and

# AT THE INTERSECTION

Many diverse identities form part of the LGBTQ+ community, and often, individuals identify with more than one term or subgroup. Members of the LGBTQ+ community may identify with terms related to gender identity (including "transgender," "agender," or "gender-fluid") or terms related to sexual orientation (such as "gay," "lesbian," "bisexual," "pansexual," or "asexual"). However, sexual orientation and gender identity are completely unrelated, and because of that, some people identify with multiple terms or identities. The overlapping of multiple minority identities is often referred to as intersectionality.

While the LGBTQ+ community has made great strides in achieving equal rights and respect, it is important to acknowledge that some subgroups within the community do not always receive the same respect and protection of their rights as others. Even within the LGBTQ+ community, there are diverse perspectives, and discrimination between subgroups exists.

However, unity with and advocacy for all members of the LGBTQ+ community is the best path toward full rights and safety. Those who are LGBTQ+ and allies alike should acknowledge and respect the many diverse identities that form the community. Together, LGBTQ+ community members are stronger.

bisexual people had to find others like them— by taking a risk. There was always the chance that a signal could be misread or that potential consequences would overshadow romance or friendship. As the nineteenth century rolled into the twentieth, more spaces for same-sex socializing began to appear, creating places where more people felt safe being out and able to make friends and pursue romantic relationships.

Whitman's gift to the future was the effect his book had on readers. The state of Massachusetts declared *Leaves of Grass* obscene because of its content in 1882, but the outcry boosted the book's popularity. Sales of the book increased, and it gained a lot of praise from critics, many of whom read the book just to find out what was so unsettling. Most importantly, there were countless gay men and lesbians who read Whitman's verse and found out that not only were they not alone, but also that their love could be something beautiful, rather than an ugly secret that should be hidden. The importance of publishing and distributing LGBTQ+ writing didn't end there.

CHAPTER TWO

# THE LOVE THAT DARE NOT SPEAK ITS NAME

●●●●●●●●●●●●●●●●●●●●●●●●●●●●●●●●●●●●●●●●●●

The gay rights movement can trace its origins to World War I. This war was a massive chain reaction of conflicts that exploded in Europe following the assassination of Austrian archduke Franz Ferdinand by a Serbian extremist group in the capital city of Bosnia. The killing activated a number of treaties and alliances that sent almost every European country into military conflict. Germany, Austria-Hungary, and the Ottoman Empire emerged as the Central Powers. Great Britain, France, Russia, Italy, and Japan formed the Allied Powers. Russia would leave the alliance following the communist uprising in 1917, the same year the United States joined the Allies.

The United States entered the war in 1917 after Britain intercepted a coded telegram from Germany asking Mexico to go to war against the United States on Germany's behalf. When the telegram was presented to American authorities, the previously neutral and isolationist country was thrust into the war during its final years. The United

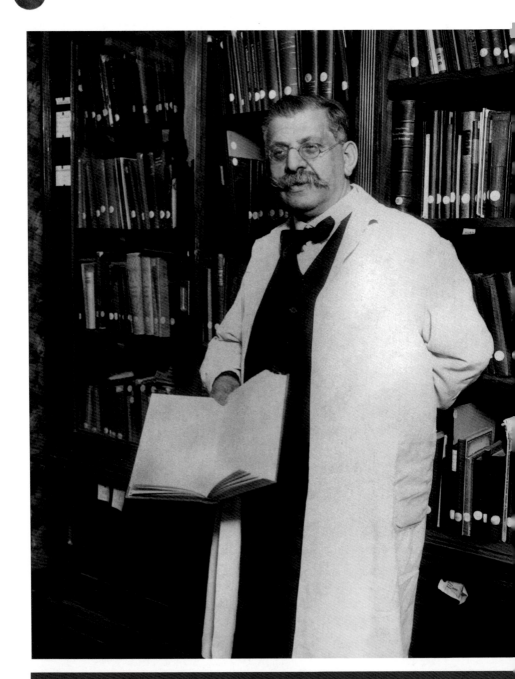

Magnus Hirschfeld (1868–1935) was a German scientist who pioneered the movement to research homosexuality objectively and scientifically.

States chose to fight alongside France and Britain against Germany and the other Central Powers.

Meanwhile, in Chicago, an immigrant named Henry Gerber was given a choice: join the American military forces fighting against his homeland of Germany or be incarcerated as an enemy alien. He chose to join the war effort.

## WELCOME STRANGER, HAPPY TO SEE YOU

Little is known about the early life of Henry Gerber. Born in Bavaria in 1892 as Josef Heinrich Dittmar, he immigrated to Chicago at age twenty-one and changed his name to Henry Gerber to sound more American. He was one of many Europeans who immigrated to Chicago in the late nineteenth and early twentieth century.

Prior to the outbreak of World War I, he had enlisted in the US Army but declared himself a conscientious objector when the United States declared war on Germany four months later. As an enemy alien, he was sent to an internment camp. According to some sources, he spent some time institutionalized for his homosexuality. After the war, he reenlisted and was stationed in Coblenz, Germany, as part of the American occupying forces. Gerber's work there involved writing and editing newspapers for the Army.

Postwar Berlin was ground zero for ideas about sex and sexuality that had been developing

# HE WHO DARED...

The event that pushed Dr. Magnus Hirschfeld to prioritize the study and support of homosexuals was the scandalous trial of Oscar Wilde. A famous writer of plays, poems, and stories, Wilde was also well known as a flamboyant personality on the London social scene.

In early 1895, the Marquess of Queensbury outed Wilde as a homosexual. Until then, Wilde had been in the closet as far as the general public was concerned. Against the advice of friends, Wilde sued the marquess for libel, which was punishable by up to two years in prison.

However, the marquess had a strategy for defense. Because of the ways in which the laws were written, the libel case could be thrown out if the offending statement was proven to be true. The marquess's attorney hired detectives to expose Wilde's private life, and during the trial they threatened to bring forth personal letters and testimonies from male prostitutes with whom Wilde had been involved. Wilde dropped the suit and was forced to repay the defendant's legal expenses.

Wilde was now not only bankrupt but was also charged with gross indecency in an extremely public and political trial. Even the marquess's attorney from the previous trial asked of the solicitor general, "Can we not let up on the poor fellow now?" Despite his attempts on the stand to defend not only himself but "the love that dare not speak its name," he was found guilty and sentenced to hard labor.

is 1878 photo shows Oscar Wilde (1854–1900) before he was outed
d convicted of gross indecency.

in Germany over the previous fifty years. The man at the forefront of this revolution was Dr. Magnus Hirschfeld. Of all the medical experts who attempted to explain homosexuality in the nineteenth century, Hirschfeld would end up having the most influence and, by comparison, the most positive and supportive approach.

Born in 1868, he originally studied philosophy before switching his focus to medicine. In the late nineteenth century, he founded the Scientific-Humanitarian Committee, a group that fought to repeal the criminalization of homosexuality and study it scientifically. Hirschfeld was part of the growing field of sexology, the study of human sexuality.

The permissive culture of Berlin in the 1920s and Hirschfeld's work were huge influences on Gerber. The economic collapse of the country after the war had a destabilizing effect on German culture. The previous conservative and militaristic aspects of society began to fall out of favor with the younger generation. Art movements such as Dadaism and expressionist cinema began to thrive, and foreign influences such as American jazz became popular.

In Berlin, Gerber found a gay culture that was unlike anything he had seen in America. There were gay bars and a thriving scene for cruising, where gay men and lesbians would go looking in public for sexual encounters with others of the same sex. Most important was Hirschfeld's institute and work, which treated homosexuality and gender nonconformity not as illnesses, but as legitimate identities.

# FIRST ITEM ON THE GAY AGENDA

When he finally returned to Chicago, Gerber was inspired by what he had seen. He convinced a few friends to form the Society for Human Rights (SHR) in 1924. This type of group would come to be known as a homophile organization. Although he conceived of the group, Gerber served only as its secretary. John T. Graves, an African American minister, was the society's president.

After electing their officers, the eight founding members wrote up an agenda for actions to take. First, they intended to ask other gay men to become members. Typical of early gay rights organizations, the society was strictly for men. Gay men and lesbians at the time were very culturally divided, and it would not be until later in the twentieth century that they began join together as a unified movement. The group excluded bisexuals, so only strictly homosexual men could be members. They also planned a series of lectures and a newsletter that would be called *Friendship and Freedom*. The group struggled, though. Without any real experience, they lacked the organizational skills and connections to get financial support from wealthy gay men.

In spite of financial struggles, excluding people who weren't gay men would prove to be the organization's downfall. The group's vice president, Al Meineger, was bisexual and married to a woman.

# WHAT'S YOUR SIGN?

During the times when gay men and lesbians had to keep their identities secret, it became important to know who else was gay and where to find safe spaces for socializing. Here are some of the secret signs and signals people came up with:

- The Hanky Code dates back to the California gold rush of the mid-nineteenth century. It began among men looking to dance in the all-male taverns that sprang up to serve the prospectors who had come looking for gold. Men would wear a handkerchief in their back left pocket if they were looking to dance with another man as the lead and one in their back right pocket if they meant to follow. A good number of these men were queer.
- In Chicago, State Street was a major thoroughfare where the many classes and cultures of the Windy City intersected. One of the signs in that neighborhood to signal that someone was gay was a red necktie. A more flamboyant color signal in early modern New York was a green suit, but the look was so flamboyant it was difficult to be discrete.
- Lesbians had their own signs and signals, too. Giving violets to another woman, inspired by a verse from the ancient Greek poet Sappho's work, was a way of admitting an attraction. In

(continued on the next page)

his 1953 portrait shows James Baldwin (1924–1987). He contributed
the canon of African American literature and to the growing body of
GBTQ+ writing.

*(continued from the previous page)*

the 1940s, some gay women would get a nautical star tattooed on their inner wrists. The trick to this was that such tattoos could be covered up with a wristwatch during the day and exposed at night.

• Books also acted as a way to find out if someone was gay. People would ask whether someone had read books such as *Giovanni's Room* by James Baldwin or Ann Bannon's *Beebo Brinker* or what they thought of gay writers such as Walt Whitman or Gertrude Stein.

Not wanting to be left out, he kept his heterosexual relationship secret. In 1925, Meineger's wife found SHR materials he had brought home. Like the members of SHR, she was completely unaware of her husband's bisexuality. She reported the evidence to police, and Graves and Gerber were both arrested. When writing about the incident later on, Gerber would mention he was showed a *Chicago Examiner* article titled "Strange Sex Cult Exposed," but that particular headline was not preserved in the paper's archives and perhaps never existed. It is more likely that the newspaper was the *Chicago American*, and the headline was "Girl Reveals Strange Cult Run by Dad."

The Gerber/Hart Library in Chicago holds these Gay Olympic Games medals and poster in its archives. The Gay Games started in 1982 in San Francisco.

Though the charges against Gerber were dropped after several trials and appeals, the legal expenses bankrupted him, and the scandal cost him his job with the post office. Despite this loss, and the failure of America's first homophile organization, he continued to write articles in support of gay rights. He took a chance and published them under his own name, rather than a pseudonym. Although his efforts with the SHR were not successful, he has been recognized and honored by the Chicago LGBTQ+ community. In 2015, his house, where the SHR held its meetings, was made a historic landmark, and the city's LGBTQ+ library, the Gerber/Hart Library, is named after him and lesbian social justice activist Pearl M. Hart.

# CHAPTER THREE

# STORM CLOUDS GATHER BEFORE THE RAINBOW

• • • • • • • • • • • • • • • • • • • • • • • • • • • • • • • • •

A s more and more gay, bisexual, and transgender people made their way into big cities, they began to shape the spaces in which they lived. The neighborhoods where they had found tolerance, or where they were able to pass, were home to immigrants and other marginalized communities. The growth of the gay community signified not only the need for more places to socialize and live, but also the need to communicate to others that they were of the same culture, sharing experiences and understanding.

As LGBTQ+-friendly neighborhoods began to emerge in major cities, there were a few common factors that helped determine where they emerged. They were usually working-class neighborhoods where the cost of living was low. In many cases, they developed in areas that were home to already-marginalized communities, which tended to be outside of the main commercial districts and therefore under less scrutiny. These areas also tended to have spaces and buildings that could be easily adapted to making gay-friendly establishments. Many of the LGBTQ+ venues from the past are gone because they were never official businesses, or they were in buildings and outdoor spaces after hours or in secret.

In New York City, the two most prominent and influential neighborhoods were Greenwich Village and Harlem.

## NEXT STOP: CHRISTOPHER STREET

By the time it was annexed to the city of New York, Greenwich Village was a town of the wealthy elite. In the early years of the twentieth century, however, the upper-class residents had moved on, and the neighborhood, then known as the Ninth Ward,

This street scene shows New York City's Greenwich Village circa 1900. This neighborhood would become a major center for LGBTQ+ activism and culture.

was home to predominantly working-class Italian immigrants. Between 1910 and 1920, the low rents led to a large number of eccentric artistic types, called bohemians, moving into the area. At the time, it was fairly isolated from the rest of the city and had a European flair.

This culture also led to a large number of gay men, lesbians, and bisexuals moving in as the Jazz Age of the twenties roared. The bohemians tended to dress extravagantly and were uninterested in conventional social norms like marriage. It was easy for gay men and lesbians to blend in there. If anyone questioned why the long-haired men or the short-haired women weren't settling down to raise a family, it would be assumed it was because they were creative types.

Gay men and lesbians were happy to be mistaken for artists, but as time went on and the Village developed a reputation, the bohemians who preceded them felt differently about being mistaken for homosexual. In 1934, the author Malcolm Cowley wrote that, as he saw it, modern art suffered from "the theory that all modern writers, painters, and musicians were homosexual."

## TAKE THE A TRAIN

Named for a city in the Netherlands, Harlem was a prominent black neighborhood by the early twentieth century. In the 1920s, the place was characterized by an arts explosion, ranging from dance to poetry,

# YOU ONLY TELL ME YOU LOVE ME WHEN YOU'RE DRUNK

When the sale and manufacture of alcoholic beverages was made illegal in 1920, secret bars opened up in major cities. Such a bar was called a speakeasy. This had a transformative effect, both positive and negative, for the gay and lesbian community.

Because all bars were now illegal—bars almost always relied on organized crime—starting one as a place for same-sex socializing and cruising was easier than it had ever been. After the end of Prohibition, many gay bars would remain associated with organized crime for decades to come and still had to make payoffs to police to avoid getting shut down. While the drinking establishments would come to function as community centers in their respective cities, the pressure to drink in order to be around other gay men and lesbians contributed to struggles with alcoholism within the community.

called the Harlem Renaissance. And as noted scholar Henry Louis Gates Jr. would write decades later, "The Harlem Renaissance was surely as gay as it was black."

## BAYARD RUSTIN: THE INVISIBLE MAN

One of the victims of Adam Clayton Powell's crusade against homosexuality was one of his own colleagues in the struggle for civil rights, Bayard Rustin. Rustin had worked for organizations such as the Fellowship of Reconciliation and the Council of Racial Equality (CORE) since moving from Pennsylvania to New York in the 1930s.

But he would leave almost every group he worked for, not because of ideological disagreements or conflicts with other members, but because he was gay. Other members, sometimes even leaders, would be nervous about the possible backlash against the movement to end segregation and overturn Jim Crow laws. Every time it came up, Rustin would voluntarily leave.

Despite this, Rustin was praised as one of the best

*(continued on the next page)*

yard Rustin (1912–1987) poses at the Citywide Committee for egration's headquarters in Brooklyn, New York. As a black man who s also gay, he held two oppressed identities.

(continued from the previous page)

organizers in the movement, and he helped develop the Southern Christian Leadership Conference (SNCC) with Martin Luther King Jr. When Powell threatened blackmail against him and King for Rustin's arrest in 1953 on a "morals charge," Rustin once again stepped down. But longtime friend and advocate A. Phillip Randolph defended him as the only man who could organize the 1963 March on Washington for Jobs and Freedom. When the group insisted Randolph oversee the event instead, he appointed Rustin as his deputy to enable him to coordinate the three hundred thousand people in attendance.

Writers such as Angelina Weld Grimké, Alain Locke, Alice Dunbar-Nelson, and Langston Hughes may have been gay or bisexual. Singer Josephine Baker divided her time between Harlem and Paris, and her heart between men and women. At the Clam House on 133rd Street, Gladys Bentley sang the blues while cross-dressing in a tuxedo, changing the lyrics of popular songs to be about loving ladies rather than gentlemen.

Adam Clayton Powell Jr. was staunchly intolerant of homosexuality. However, he was also an important figure in the struggle for African American rights.

The neighborhood wasn't just for artistic celebrities; there was a culture of tolerance and acceptance that many took advantage of. "You did what you wanted to," said artist and writer Richard Bruce Nugent. "Nobody was in the closet. There wasn't any closet." In many of the famous venues of the time, such as the Cotton Club, same-sex and straight couples shared the space, and the annual drag ball at the Hamilton Lodge was one of the biggest events in Harlem. Soon enough, many were involved. Thousands came to see performances by male and female impersonators—and some of the audience cross-dressed, too. Gay and bisexual women may have been more public about their relationships with other women, but they could still be criticized and verbally attacked for turning down the attentions of male suitors.

But not everyone was as accepting of such lifestyles. Adam Clayton Powell, then a Baptist pastor in Harlem, spoke out and campaigned against what he saw as a perversion of morality. Although he would go on to be a major figure within the civil rights movement, he would remain unaccepting of homosexuals.

Many claims and accusations have been made against historians who have intentionally or otherwise obscured the queer legacy of the Harlem Renaissance. Other ways the past has been rewritten have come in the form of legal action by the families and estates of public figures who have wanted to avoid their reputations being "tarnished."

## NO ONE IS EVER ALLOWED TO HAVE ANY FUN EVER AGAIN

One of the strongest opponents of the emerging gay culture was the New York Society for the Suppression of Vice (NYSSV). Founded in 1873 by Anthony Comstock, NYSSV was dedicated to enforcing city laws on moral conduct and opposing "obscene" content. Comstock was also responsible for lobbying for laws prohibiting "obscene, lewd, lascivious, or filthy" printed material from being delivered by the US Postal Service. Gay rights advocates from Henry Gerber onward would struggle against these restrictions.

During the 1920s and 1930s, as more gay, bisexual, and transgender people found outlets for their voices in art, the NYSSV used public pressure to censor and fine writers and artists. Its complaints against Edouard Boulet's play *The Captive*, one of the first Broadway shows with lesbian themes, led the state legislature to pass a "padlock bill." Under this bill, the police were allowed to padlock the doors of a theater where "obscene" plays were being staged.

The British writer Radclyffe Hall's *The Well of Loneliness* was the first popular novel to address

Anthony Comstock (1844–1915) founded the New York Society for the Suppression of Vice in 1873. It was enabled and at least partially funded by the New York State legislature.

female homosexuality. When it came out in 1928, England promptly banned it. A year later, when it arrived in America, eight hundred copies were seized by the NYSSV, and the society's secretary, John S. Sumner, began a push to have it banned in the United States, as it had been in Britain. However, after two months, the case was appealed, and the book was found not to have been written in an obscene manner. Hall herself was anything but scandalous and was actually quite conservative politically. She kept her distance from the early feminist movements of the time.

As time went on, the NYSSV found itself being challenged and losing more and more often. It also found that trying to ban works of art that discussed homosexuality often brought negative attention and publicity to them.

# CHAPTER FOUR

# FROM SPECIAL FRIENDS TO BROTHERS IN ARMS

• • • • • • • • • • • • • • • • • • • • • • • • • • • • • • • • • • •

I n 1961, a letter would be published in one of the gay periodicals from a veteran named Brian Keith. In it he wrote:

> *This is in memory of an anniversary—the anniversary of October 27th, 1943, when I first heard you singing in North Africa. That song brings memories of the happiest times I have ever known. Memories of a GI show troop... and a handsome boy with a wonderful tenor voice... The happiness when told we were going home—and the misery when we learned that we would not be going together. Fond goodbyes on a secluded beach beneath the star-studded velvet of an African night, and the tears that would not be stopped as I stood atop the sea-wall and watched your convoy disappear over the horizon.*

Many shared Keith's experience. In fact, the military conflict known as World War II had a major transformative effect on the lives and culture of gay men and women. In many ways, the war accelerated the advancement of the gay rights movement.

## WORLD WAR II BEGINS

This global conflict began in 1939, when Germany, under the leadership of Adolf Hitler's Nazi Party, invaded neighboring Poland. Prior to this, the government had begun militarizing the country and instituting strict policies of institutional racism that saw Germans of Jewish faith, Romani people, Catholics, and socialists arrested and sent to concentration camps, where they were either worked to death or killed in mass executions.

Homosexuals were also victims of the Nazis. The purges started in the mid-1930s when gay bars were shut down, and homosexual men and women were required to wear pink triangles sewn onto their clothes to identify them. This was both so they could be easily rounded up when the camps were ready to accept them and to make them stand out. Individual citizens were not the only victims, as Magnus Hirschfeld's institute and all of his research were destroyed. Sadly, when the war was over and the camps were liberated, the tens of thousands of gay men and

Many materials that Nazis and Hitler Youth determined to be hostile to the interests of Germany were gathered in a truck and brought to the Opernplatz in Berlin to be burned in public.

women who had survived were sent to prison, as homosexuality was still criminalized under section 175 of the German penal code.

## MANUFACTURING A WAR

The United States entered the war in 1941 (it would end in 1945) when the Japanese air force attacked the Pearl Harbor naval base in Honolulu, Hawaii. Japan was an ally of Germany, so after the attack, Hitler declared war on the United States. The United States was now fighting on two sides of the world in what were called the European and the Pacific theaters of war.

Both men and women were in demand for the war effort. Men would serve primarily

US troops are seen here crossing the German front line in Roetgen, circa 1944. On September 2, 1945, the war ended.

as soldiers, pilots, and sailors. Although women were not put into combat, they were vital both at home and abroad. Women were employed in administrative capacities and worked in intelligence analysis for the military and took over what had historically been male jobs in the United States. Many women also ended up working for military intelligence as code breakers who used complex mathematics to decipher enemy communications.

The demand for women in industry and other jobs offered three things that allowed women, gay and straight, a level of independence they had never had before. First, it gave single

## Discharge from The Army of the United States

### TO ALL WHOM IT MAY CONCERN:

This is to Certify, That* _____ NORMAN F. SANSOM

† _12203359, Private, Walterboro Base Detachment, Walterboro, South Carolina_

THE ARMY OF THE UNITED STATES is hereby DISCHARGED from military service of the UNITED STATES by reason of ‡ _Section VIII, AR 615-_ _not eligible for reenlistment, induction, or reinduction, per 2nd Ind. Hqs._ _Columbia Army Air Base, Columbia, South Carolina dated December 21, 1943._

Said _Norman F. Sansom_ _____, in the State of _Connecticut_ was in _Bridgeport_ _____. When enlisted he was _20 8/12_ years of age and by occupation a _IBM Operator_. He had _Blue_ eyes, _Brown_ hair, _Ruddy_ complexion, was _5_ feet _11_ inches in height.

Given under my hand at _Walterboro Army Air Field, Walterboro, S.C._ ____ day of _January_ ____, one thousand nine hundred and ____

_William M._ _____
WILLIAM H. PRINE

Started in 1916, the blue discharge was used during World War II to remove homosexuals from military service. It was also used under other circumstances.

women an excuse to leave home and move to another city without having to get married. It also gave them the chance to acquire skills and earn money. Lastly, especially for gay women, it enabled them to form romantic and platonic relationships with other women.

Gay men had similar opportunities, but with greater risks of injury or death from fighting enemy soldiers. For many of them, though, their deployment allowed them to visit big cities like New York and find other gay men in bars and bathhouses.

## LEAVING OUT GAY SERVICEMEN

While big cities offered more venues for gay socializing, the military had been influenced by the growing study of psychology. While homosexuality had been seen as a form of criminal action decades earlier, it was coming to be seen as a mental ailment. Recruits were subjected to psychological examinations to determine if they had gay tendencies. If they were found to have them, they could be discharged as mentally unfit.

Generally, at the end of their service, military personnel were discharged, meaning they were no longer active and could return to civilian status. Most received an honorable discharge, which entitled them to benefits ranging from medical coverage to college tuition. However, if a soldier was found guilty by court martial of a serious crime, he or she would be dishonorably discharged, stripped of benefits, and labeled as a convicted felon in some states.

George Washington issued the first dishonorable discharge in American history during the American Revolution. Lieutenant Frederick Gotthold Enslin had been found guilty of sodomy in 1778. A diary account from the time describes him having his coat turned inside out as he was exiled from the military camp in which he had served.

During World War II, because time and manpower were limited, men and women found guilty of homosexual behavior were issued a blue discharge. Blue discharges were considered neither honorable nor dishonorable. Unlike a dishonorable discharge, there was no military trial, so accused individuals had no opportunity to defend themselves. Although it did not include criminal sentencing, it did revoke a soldier's veteran's benefits and served as a permanent legal record of his "non-dishonorable offense." Many gay and bisexual soldiers from small towns or rural areas felt unable to return to their communities, fearing shame because of their discharges, and instead stayed in the big cities such as New York City and San Francisco when they returned from overseas.

## QUEER AND IN WAR

Those who evaded being outed while serving in the military didn't have an easy time, either. In deployment cities like New York City and San Francisco, the military exercised Vice Control Powers (VCP) that allowed military police to follow soldiers off base, as well as stand guard outside and inside of known gay bars. Of course, this also made it easy for gay soldiers to find such places. All they had to do was look for the man in uniform standing guard.

Illegal operations called locker clubs sprang up in the cities. In these places, a serviceman could pay a small fee to store his uniform in a locker and change into civilian clothes to evade detection. Without a uniform, they could walk right past the guards and go enjoy a drink with other gay men—provided the guard didn't recognize them from the base.

In the field of combat, it could go either way. If soldiers were exposed as gay, they could be sent to the stockades, which were military jails.

By contrast, some commanding officers saw their women and men as more valuable in service than in jail and so looked the other way.

After the war, thousands of gay and bisexual men and women returned to the United States, arriving by the boatload in the same big cities from which they had deployed. Many of them chose to stay where they landed, and almost overnight the gay populations of those cities exploded. Even those who returned to midsized cities were changed by their experience, and smaller cities began to see the opening of more gay and lesbian bars.

This photo shows soldiers in New York City's Penn Station in August 1942. The United States had entered World War II just eight months earlier.

Drinking establishments weren't the only new thing to open up after the war. A small group of honorably discharged gay veterans in New York City joined together to form the Veterans Benevolent Association (VBA), an organization designed to provide support for its members while they adjusted to civilian life after the horrors of the war. It closed in 1954, but the VBA was one of the first major progay organizations in the United States—albeit one restricted to military veterans.

# CHAPTER FIVE

# A THIN LINE BETWEEN LOVE AND CRIME

● ● ● ● ● ● ● ● ● ● ● ● ● ● ● ● ● ● ● ● ● ● ● ● ● ● ● ● ● ● ● ● ● ● ● ● ● ● ● ● ●

In the aftermath of World War II, a new conflict arose between the United States and the Soviet Union, the likes of which hadn't been seen before. Both countries had strong militaries and were ideologically opposed between American capitalism and Soviet communism. But neither of them wanted to risk a full-blown war. The two countries entered a decades-long period of stalemate called the Cold War, a byproduct of which was the red scare in America.

The objective of the scare was to prevent communism from developing both within and outside the United States. Leftist politics came under suspicion, and any criticism of American policy could be seen as a hostile act. Senator Joseph McCarthy was the most vocal voice in this climate of fear, making claims that he had evidence of hundreds of communists working within the government. The House Un-American Activities Committee (HUAC), a group that served to root out dissent against US policy, expelled thousands of people from their jobs in the federal government.

Many artists, especially those in Hollywood, were blacklisted for suspected communist sympathies and unable to find work. Part of what made the scare so far reaching was the idea that anyone could be a communist or communist sympathizer.

## THE LAVENDER SCARE

The government also orchestrated a witch hunt against gay people. As homosexuality came to be seen as a disease rather than a crime, politicians, journalists, and laymen began to fear that gay men and lesbians secretly lurked among them. This was known as the lavender scare. In many ways, this was a continuation of the purging of gay men, lesbians, and bisexuals from military service during the war, only broadened to the whole federal government. Executive Order 10450 required a thorough investigation of any federal government worker in the name of national security. Homosexuality was considered a threat and could therefore be grounds for dismissal from government jobs.

These investigations and laws forced gay men, lesbians, and bisexuals to conceal their sexuality even more than was common in the general population. Rumors alone were enough for someone to be brought under suspicion, and in order to defend themselves, people's whole lives would come under scrutiny. Even if no proof could be determined, there was still the scandal

President Dwight D. Eisenhower (1890–1969) is shown here at the White House in 1955. Under his administration, homosexuality became grounds for dismissal from federal jobs.

of being investigated. After all, if someone was straight, why would they have been suspected in the first place? Homosexuals were characterized as mentally ill and morally unstable, and they were considered a security liability because they were at risk of being blackmailed. A closeted homosexual, the reasoning went, could be forced by foreign agents to divulge national secrets under the threat of exposure.

Although there was no blacklist in Hollywood for gay men and lesbians, the hostile climate of general homophobia created a fear of unemployment that kept many actors, screenwriters, and directors in the closet. The Motion Picture Production Hollywood Code of 1930, also called the Hays Code, stated that movies must maintain certain moral standards that, in effect, prohibited any depictions of homosexuality onscreen. The code was repealed in the late 1950s, and by the 1960s, material that had been banned was making its way back on screen. But even then, portrayals of queer people were uniformly negative. Such characters were portrayed as psychologically damaged or manipulative criminals. LGBTQ+ characters often died by the end of a movie, either in an accident, by suicide, or by murder. The same was true of literature of the time. Early fictional portrayals of homosexual, bisexual, or transgender people were considered scandalous. In an attempt to deflect accusations of promoting homosexuality, a publisher might even go so far as to claim that novels with these characters were meant as a psychological examination of the "homosexual illness."

Patricia Highsmith (1921–1995), a successful author of crime novels, wrote the lesbian love story *The Price of Salt* under a pen name so that her writing career wouldn't suffer.

Despite this, a number of novels with gay and bisexual content came out during this time, such as Gore Vidal's *The City and the Pillar*, James Baldwin's *Giovanni's Room*, and John Rechy's *City of Night*. *The Price of Salt* (1952), credited to Claire Morgan, tells the story of a young woman who begins a relationship with a married woman going through a divorce. The book was radical for the time, in

# THE FIRST PUBLIC TRANSGENDER HERO

Christine Jorgensen, designated male at birth, was born in New York City in 1926 as George Jorgensen Jr. She would later describe her childhood as happy, but as she grew older the feeling of being a woman in a man's body frustrated her. During World War II, she served in the army and was honorably discharged. After returning to civilian life, she decided to seek gender affirmation surgery, then a radical new procedure, at the age of twenty-four.

Jorgensen's transition, which began with two years of hormone therapy, was completed in 1952 with the gender affirmation surgery performed in Denmark by Dr. Christian Hamburger. On her return to the United States in 1955, she made headlines in the daily tabloids and even in newspapers like the *New York*

*Times.* Jorgensen was public about her transitional procedures and was the first transgender person to discuss them publicly. She later went on tour to give lectures and perform in clubs, where her signature song became "I Enjoy Being a Girl."

that its two female lovers are happily together at the end of the book. When the novel was reprinted in 1990, it was revealed to have been written by popular mystery author Patricia Highsmith, who had originally published the book using a pseudonym.

## A ZOOLOGIST WALKS INTO A SOCIOLOGY CLASS...

In the middle of all this, one of the most important developments in the gay rights movement happened. It did not come from a homophile organization, but it came, in fact, from a class on marriage at Indiana University taught by, of all people, a zoologist.

Alfred Kinsey was born in Hoboken, New Jersey, in 1894 to a Methodist family with Quaker roots. He was often ill, and his family lived in poverty. Because of his illness, he was unable to play rough with the other boys, who consequently looked down on him as being too meek.

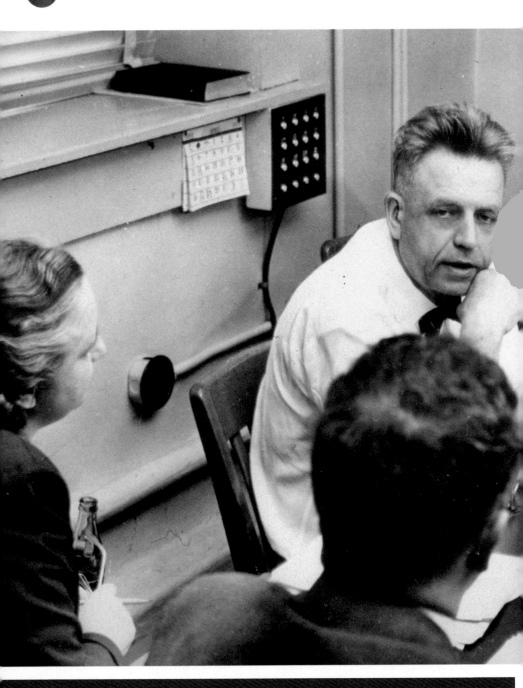

Alfred Kinsey (*center, facing camera*) and his staff are shown here at work in 1953.

Graduating from Harvard in 1919 with a doctorate in biology, Kinsey had focused his studies on insects and went on to become a respected professor in zoology. It was while teaching at Indiana University in 1938 that he discovered how much misinformation his students had about sex and sexuality and how little scientific research there was about it.

This led Kinsey to begin researching sexual behavior. He was not the first person to study sex. Magnus Hirschfeld preceded him, as did nineteenth-century sexologists such as Richard von Krafft-Ebbing and Henry Havelock Ellis. However, Kinsey was the first to approach the field with rigorous scientific methodology.

# THE KINSEY SCALE

In 1944, Kinsey applied for and received a grant from the Rockefeller Foundation that allowed him to conduct a series of interviews with more than five thousand men. These interviews asked a wide range of questions about their sexual experiences and beliefs. The results were published in 1948 in the book *Sexual Behavior in the Human Male*, and the results were shocking.

Kinsey had proven through a scientific collection of data that much of what was considered obscure or deviant behavior at the time was actually fairly common. Of the men interviewed, it was found that 37 percent had experienced satisfactory sex with other men; 10 percent were exclusively homosexual; and 50 percent experienced sexual attraction to other men. His findings also suggested that bisexuality was more common than previously thought.

Kinsey also established from his research the idea of a scale of sexuality, called the Kinsey scale. He presented a scale of 0 (strictly heterosexual) to 6 (strictly homosexual), with five different degrees of bisexuality in between.

The book was controversial, yet also very popular. It became a best-seller. Kinsey's strongly objective methodology made the book a public spectacle. Every statistic he presented could be backed up by thorough research and analysis. Refining his research methods further, in 1953 he released *Sexual Behavior in the Human Female*, which revealed similar statistics about his female subjects.

By this point, Kinsey and his work were upsetting a lot of people, so much so that religious leaders and conservative politicians pressured the Rockefeller Foundation to cut his funding. Kinsey was also branded as an anti-American subversive with communist sympathies. Kinsey was unable to publish his research. He died in 1956 of pneumonia and heart problems.

## THE VALUE AND SHORTCOMINGS OF KINSEY'S WORK

There are some criticisms concerning Kinsey's work. His interview subjects were almost uniformly white and middle class, as well as predominantly American, and there were not any transgender subjects included in the interviews. Additionally, his statistics were taken from a comparatively small group of subjects. While his research did challenge existing ideas about sexuality, they are not a terminal analysis of human sexuality as a whole.

However, his research gave scientific evidence that revealed heterosexuality in a new light, and rather than being viewed as an aberration, homosexuality and bisexuality proved to be much more prevalent than once thought. His work helped change the way people looked at homosexuals and bisexuals and enabled the ongoing field of research on sexuality and gender. Kinsey broke the dominant narrative of "deviant sexuality" as being pathological. He further normalized the idea of queer identities when he wrote:

> *If all persons with any trace of homosexual history, or those who were predominantly homosexual, were eliminated from the population today, there is no reason for believing that the incidence of the homosexual in the next generation would be materially reduced. The homosexual has been a significant part of human sexuality ever since the dawn of history, primarily because it is an expression of capacities that are basic in the human animal.*

In other words, the existence of gay and queer people cannot be eradicated because non-heteronormative sexualities cannot be predicted or prevented. But it is not abnormal to hold such an identity, and it is not a new state of being.

# CHAPTER SIX

# COMING TOGETHER WHILE STANDING APART

· · · · · · · · · · · · · · · · · · · · · · · · · · · · · · · · · · · · · · · · ·

The red scare and lavender scare of the 1950s defined communists and homosexuals as bogeymen in order to frighten and intimidate the American public into tolerating and enabling purges in government and the arts. Part of what made both witch hunts so effective was that *anyone* could be accused of being a communist or homosexual, and the accused were guilty until proven innocent. Harry Hays found a unique way to avoid accusations: he embraced them. He was both an out homosexual and a card-carrying member of the American Communist Party.

Born in England, Hays and his family moved to California after his father was severely injured in a factory accident. During the summer, he would work on a ranch in Nevada. There he was introduced to the economic ideas of Karl Marx after his encounters with members of the International Workers of the World (IWW), a labor rights organization. The main ideas of Marxist philosophy, both politically and in terms of collective organization, would become major influences on him and part of the founding ideas of the new homophile movement to come.

## THAT WAS THEN, THIS IS NOW

As a communist and a gay man, Hays understood that the purges Senator McCarthy led were targeting people like him on both sides of his life. Under the scares of the 1950s, people lost their jobs, were socially shunned, and suffered financial loss. What Hays saw was that the people targeted had no networks of support when they were under investigation. At the same time, he was also paying attention to the actions and successes of the civil rights movement under leaders such as Martin Luther King Jr., John Lewis, and Bayard Rustin.

A third influence came when Hays met someone who claimed to have been a member of the

The Mattachine Society founder Harry Hay (1912–2002) (*third from left*) appears at a press conference at the Stonewall Inn on the twenty-fifth anniversary of the Stonewall riots.

Society for Human Rights. Hays had never heard of this group. No one had, as there was no public history of the SHR, save for a newspaper article describing it as a cult. Hays found Henry Gerber's vision inspiring. With his organizational background, he believed he could make it work.

Along with Chuck Rowland, Dale Jennings, and Bob Hull, Hays formed the Mattachine Foundation in Los Angeles in 1951. The goals of the foundation were to bring gay people together, provide education and leadership, and encourage political action. Possibly inspired by the circumstances of how their predecessors had been shut down, they used a cell structure for the organization. As they gained new members and opened new chapters in other cities, members knew only the identities of the other members of their individual cells. So if a group in San Diego was compromised, the arresting authorities would not have any information with which to pursue groups in other cities.

Not everyone in the foundation was happy with the strong Marxist ideals of Hays, though. In 1953, there was a break within the group. The founding leaders were removed and replaced with new officers. The group became more conservative in its politics and actions, and it was renamed the Mattachine Society. Four years later, the society moved operations to San Francisco.

The Mattachine Society was both influential and successful. Chapters began in major cities, including Boston, Detroit, Denver, and New York, before disbanding. But just as the society was closing down nationally, its Washington, DC, chapter started up, and the society wasn't about to call it quits just yet. Frank Kameny, who had been a victim of the previous decade's panics and purges, led the DC group. Kameny had been an astronomer with the US Army Map Service until he was outed as a gay man.

Under Kameny's direction, the DC chapter took a different approach from the West Coast founders. While Hays was influenced by Marxist communism, Kameny used the language and reasoning from his study of constitutional rights. He and his community became very skilled and effective at lobbying the US government on their own terms—up to and including writing to President John F. Kennedy requesting that homosexuality be decriminalized.

## THE INTERNATIONAL GAY AND LESBIAN ARCHIVE

An offshoot of the Mattachine Society was a side organization called ONE Inc. Members of the society felt that a different kind of organization was needed to better promote educational goals. The group began by publishing a magazine, called *ONE*, which debuted in 1953 and ran until 1968.

*(continued on the next page)*

*(continued from the previous page)*

Among *ONE*'s most prolific writers was Jim Kepner. Kepner was born in 1923 and left his adoptive family at the age of nineteen to move to San Francisco, where he had learned a gay and lesbian community was beginning to flourish. Kepner loved to read, and shortly after he moved to the city he began collecting books about gay men and lesbians. These included cheap paperback novels and psychological and medical books.

His collection continued to grow long after World War II. In the 1950s, he acquired a huge collection of newspaper clippings and magazine articles, and in 1954 he started writing articles himself. Kepner published more than 1,600 articles. His personal collection, which he named the Western Gay Archive, was made open to the public in 1979. The name was changed to ONE National Gay & Lesbian Archives when the collection moved to the University of Southern California in 2000. Today the archive consists of more than two million books, magazines, and newspapers, as well as video and audio recordings, photographs, artwork, and more. It is one of the largest collections of LGBTQ+ materials in the world.

## SISTERS DOING IT FOR THEMSELVES

Just as gay men and women returning from Europe after World War II settled in New York City, San Francisco, California, was the main port of return from the Pacific theater. By the 1950s, the North

This 1965 photo shows Dick Leitsch (1935–) at the Mattachine Society's East Coast location. Leitsch became the president of the Mattachine Society in the 1960s.

Beach neighborhood had become the place to be if you were gay. There were several prominent bars, meetings and parties held in private homes, and an ample amount of socializing and cruising in the parks and on the beaches.

But for as much gay life as there was, it was still pushed to the margins. Dancing in gay bars was prohibited, and raids by the police were frequent. It was this lack of safe spaces that gave Rose Bamberger, a Filipino woman, the idea to found a social club for lesbians. Together with seven other women, Bamberger formed the Daughters of Bilitis (DOB) in 1955. The name came from a poem by Pierre Louys called "The Songs of Bilitis," which was a tribute to the famous Greek poet Sappho, who had written of love between women thousands of years ago.

The founding membership was remarkably diverse, with half the members coming from working-class backgrounds and the other half being more middle class. During the first few meetings, it was decided the club colors were blue and gold, and that the club pin would be in the shape of a triangle. Out of the original eight, Del Martin and Phyllis Lyon were elected to leadership positions.

It was decided that the DOB was to be a women-only group that would reflect the struggles of both women and homosexuals. New members had to be sponsored by one of the founding members, homosexual, female, and of "good moral character." Members also had to be twenty-one years of age or older, as the group wanted to avoid being seen as interacting with minors.

The poet Sappho (c. 630–c. 570 BCE) wrote verse about love between women over 2,500 years ago. She lived on the island of Lesbos, which is where the word "lesbian" comes from.

After several meetings, Martin called for new rules, including a dress code. Out of concern that prospective members might be scared off by women appearing too "butch," or masculine presenting, strictly feminine attire was enforced. "If slacks are to be worn," stated the new rules, "they must be women's slacks."

## SEE HOW THEY RISE UP

One of the ways the DOB reached out to the community was through its newsletter, *The Ladder*. Its name came from the notion that the publication would help lesbians rise up, becoming both publicly visible and more mobile socially. Beginning in 1956, the journal published news and essays about homosexual and women's issues, along with poetry and fiction. This combination of art and reportage offered many different ways to explore and express lesbian identity.

In an attempt to make connections between the organization and female professionals, staffers looked up

In 2004, Phyllis Lyon (*left*) and Del Martin (*right*) were the first same-sex couple to be married in San Francisco. In 1955, they founded the Daughters of Bilitis, the first organization for homosexual women.

the addresses of all the female lawyers in San Francisco in the telephone directory (books that contained telephone numbers and addresses for both private citizens and public businesses). Copies of the second issue were mailed to every woman practicing law in the city. Many were angered by this unsolicited mailing and demanded to be removed from the mailing list. Some of them were angry because the mailings insinuated that they were gay when they were not. Some were gay but in the closet, and they were eager to keep their personal and private lives separate. But not all the responses were negative, and the DOB did gain some new members from the stunt.

The Ladder became a very important publication for gay women. Up until it ceased publication in 1972, it supported cooperation with scientific research on sexuality, encouraged members to write regularly to their legislators, and provided an outlet for many lesbian writers to begin publishing.

The presence of organizations like the Daughters of Bilitis, the Mattachine Society, and ONE Inc. helped to shape the character of California (especially San Francisco) as a progressive and inclusive place for gay men and lesbians. The combination of activism and social spaces offered a diversity of lifestyle possibilities. This environment also helped form the idea that the recreational and political sides of homosexual society didn't have to be in conflict with each other. Activist groups offered an alternative to the bar scene, but they also helped to protect and support the bars.

# CHAPTER SEVEN

# THE ROAD TO STONEWALL

· · · · · · · · · · · · · · · · · · · · · · · · · · · · · · · · · · · · · · ·

During the 1950s and 1960s, the organized movement for gay rights gained a massive amount of momentum. Where previous collective efforts mainly raised awareness of the existence of LGBTQ+ identities and offered self-help, LGBTQ+ people soon began to demand more, specifically the public stamp of legitimacy and validation of the community's legal rights.

## FROM THE STAGE TO THE VOTING BOOTH

In the early 1950s, a young Latino man named José Sarria started performing in drag and soon changed the face of San Francisco politics. A veteran of World War II, Sarria had returned to San Francisco, his hometown, to teach at a local college. But shortly after getting hired, he was arrested in the men's bathroom of a local hotel on a charge of solicitation. Now with a record as a sex criminal, he was let go from his job and unable to find work as a teacher.

A drag queen friend suggested Sarria apply to work at a local tavern called the Black Cat Café, known for its gay clientele and female impersonation shows. At first, he started out waiting tables before trying out onstage. Sarria was a hit. Soon he was performing three times a night. He became a fixture of the club and helped transform the café into a center for LGBTQ+ socializing and organizing.

In 1961, he ran for the office of city supervisor under the slogan "Gay is good!" He didn't actually plan to win. The goal was to promote voter solidarity among gay men and lesbians. No one in city government expected a gay Latino who performed in drag and had no political experience to have a chance of winning.

But on the final day to apply to run, city officials made a shocking discovery: they had five seats on the Board of Supervisors to fill but fewer than five candidates. It wouldn't matter how many votes Sarria got because without any other candidates, this gay Latino who performed in drag and had no political experiences would be, technically, unopposed.

In a panic, city officials scrambled to get people to apply to run. A total of thirty-four candidates ran for Board of Supervisors, 90 percent of whom were last-minute additions. While they did manage to block Sarria from joining the board, he came in ninth with about six thousand votes, beating out twenty-five other candidates. Suddenly, the LGBTQ+ voters were a demographic with rising power. José Sarria may not have won his campaign,

Harvey Milk (1930–1978) talks to the media in San Francisco on October 20, 1978. José Sarria's 1961 run for office as an openly gay candidate paved the way for Milk to become the first openly gay elected official in 1978.

but he helped pave the way for LGBTQ+ inclusion in San Francisco politics.

## STANDING UP AND COMING OUT

In the 1940s, the gay population of Seattle began to grow as airplane manufacturing brought in large numbers of men to work assembling fighter planes and bombers. Then, when the men were sent to war, the women came in and filled the jobs they left behind. Both communities were homosocial, with same-sex living arrangements, socializing, and work communities. After the war, many of the people who'd migrated from elsewhere in the country stayed.

By the late 1950s, two of the city's most prominent gay bars were the Blue Note and the Madison Tavern. As in other cities, payoffs by establishments to police were a common thing, but that suddenly changed. When MacIver Wells, owner

At the time of Sarria's campaign, George Christopher (*pictured*) was the mayor of San Francisco. He was the last Republican mayor of that city.

of the Madison Tavern, went to make his regular payoff to the police, he was told the deal was off and that no money could be taken while an investigation was ongoing.

Three weeks later, with no warning, police raids started up at both the Madison Tavern and the nearby Blue Note. The latter was owned by James G. Watson. The police told patrons of both bars to show identification and answer questions. The bars were sometimes raided twice in one night. Attendance dropped off, and the bars went from increasing profits to losing money.

Both owners were frustrated. Their businesses were suffering, and because they couldn't make payoffs to avoid harassment, they had no recourse to protest the constant police raids—except one.

On October 9, 1958, Watson and Wells filed a lawsuit against the city of Seattle, claiming that the police were harassing their patrons without just cause and costing them revenue. As part of the suit, they demanded that the city reimburse them for the profits they had lost.

This was unheard of! Gay bars had been raided for decades and had never fought back in the courts. This had largely been because the majority of gay bars were owned by organized crime. But Wells and Watson owned their establishments outright; they were legitimate businessmen. As the proceedings went on, the city was unprepared to go to trial. It was unclear that the city could prove that the bar's activities justified the police raids.

The city of Seattle agreed to settle out of court, and on November 19, the charges were dropped. The police would stay out of the Blue Note and the Madison Tavern unless they had a legitimate reason to investigate. The raids were officially over. In return, Wells and Watson dropped their request to be repaid for lost revenue.

## THE ROAD TO STONEWALL

Much changed in America for LGBTQ+ people in the 1960s. Police raids of gay bars were slowly becoming less frequent. Homosexuality was becoming discussed not in hushed whispers but in professional dialogues. And most significantly, the number of gay and lesbian organizations was rapidly growing.

Many of the LGBTQ+ groups were additional chapters of existing groups such as the Mattachine Society and the Daughters of Bilitis, but there were a number of new groups popping up as well. Some of these groups were taking a different approach to the same message and goals, like the Janus Society. Others, like the Council on Religion and the Homosexual, focused on addressing gay issues in specific cultural areas. And it wasn't just in the United States that the movement was gaining traction. The first Canadian homophile organization, the Association for Social Knowledge, started up in 1964. Mexico faced struggles in a different cultural context and would not begin to form homophile organizations until the late 1960s and early 1970s.

New York City was undergoing a lot of progress. The city's Civil Service Commission made public

# DESPITE SOCIAL PROGRESS...

Negative categorization of gay men and lesbians was still a battlefield. The American Psychiatric Association (APA) had published a book in 1952 called the *Diagnostic and Statistical Manual of Mental Disorders (DSM)*. The book offered a system of classification and categorization for diagnosing mental illnesses and disorders.

In the first edition, homosexuality was labeled as a sociopathic personality disorder, meaning that gay men and lesbians were unfit for social interaction within their existing culture. In the second edition of the *DSM*, released in 1968, homosexuality had been rebranded as a "non-psychotic mental disorder." What this meant was that gay men, lesbians, and bisexual people who were arrested could be labeled incompetent and lose some of their rights in legal proceedings ranging from criminal sentencing to divorce and custody suits. Years of protests finally led to homosexuality as a mental disorder being fully removed from the *DSM* in 1987.

that it would not discriminate against gay men and lesbians in its hiring. The State Liquor Commission had stated on record that serving gay people drinks didn't violate the law. The last straw to break to bring about the cessation of police raids on gay bars came when the city courts ruled that it was not illegal for same-sex partners to dance together.

All of this set the scene for the bar raid that would transform the gay rights movement and lead to the modern intersectional LGBTQ+ movement. On the night of June 27, 1969, police raided the Stonewall Inn, a bar in New York City's Greenwich Village. The Stonewall was owned by organized crime who ran the bar without a liquor license. The pretext of the raid was the bar's many building code violations, but to the patrons inside it was harassment that they thought had been eradicated. What tipped the raid into a riot was that while patrons were being ejected, transgender patrons were being arrested. Cross-dressing was still criminalized under local law.

While the gay, bisexual, and transgender people outside the bar had begun pelting the police with pennies, it is believed that transgender women of color, by most accounts including African American Marsha P. Johnson and Puerto Rican Sylvia Rivera, threw the first bottles. The police became overwhelmed as members of the LGBTQ+ community and their supporters amassed outside, and they eventually had to barricade themselves inside the bar. Conflicts between the police and the LGBTQ+

On June 24, 2016, President Barack Obama designated the Stonewall Inn a national monument. The bar displays memorabilia commemorating the night of the riots.

THIS IS A
RAIDED
PREMISES

POLICE DEP'T.
:ITY OF NEW YORK
OWARD R. LEARY. POLICE COMMISSIONER

community lasted for three days. Craig Rodwell, an activist and participant in the riots, was quoted as saying, "People often ask what was special about that night—there was no one thing special about it. It was just everything coming together, one of those moments in history that is: you were there, you know this is it, this is what we've been waiting for."

A month after the riots, bisexual activist Brenda Howard organized a liberation march in the Stonewall neighborhood, celebrated as Christopher Street Liberation Day. The next year's march is considered to be the nation's first pride

# THE FORGOTTEN UPRISING

While the Stonewall uprising is considered to be the major turning point in LGBTQ+ history, it was not the first time the community had clashed with police.

A popular place for the transgender community in San Francisco's Tenderloin district was Compton's Cafeteria, part of a chain of inexpensive eateries in the city owned by Gene Compton. Transgender women and some gay men and women would use this particular location as a place to gather and socialize because the gay bars at the time did not allow transgender people admission. The owners of the restaurant were often hostile toward them as well and called the police.

In August 1966, the police were called in and began roughly handling transgender patrons. Suddenly, one of the women threw a cup of hot coffee in the face of an officer, and a fight broke out between the police and the LGBTQ+ patrons. Police officers were assaulted, windows were smashed, and a nearby newsstand was burned to the ground.

In the days that followed, protests against both the police and Compton's Cafeteria were led by the recently formed activist group Vanguard, which supported transgender people and was also concerned with poverty and homelessness among LGBTQ+ people. The riot is considered a turning point for transgender activism. Unfortunately, it is often ignored in gay and lesbian histories, many of which choose to emphasize the Stonewall riots as the first time LGBTQ+ people collectively fought back against oppression.

parade. Since then, LGBTQ+ pride has traditionally been celebrated on the last Sunday in June. The Stonewall uprising was the catalyzing event that began to unite transgender people, bisexuals, lesbians, and gay men together. It transformed their separate struggles and conflicts into the modern LGBTQ+ movement.

# TIMELINE

**1855** Walt Whitman's *Leaves of Grass*, which describes romantic attraction between men, is published.

**1882** The state of Massachusetts declares *Leaves of Grass* obscene.

**1895** Oscar Wilde is sentenced to two years of hard labor for gross indecency.

**1924** The Society for Human Rights, the first homophile organization in the United States, is founded in Chicago.

**1925** The Society for Human Rights is disbanded after a police raid leads to the arrests of founder Henry Gerber and the group's president, John T. Graves. A newspaper exposé publicly disparages the group as a cult.

**1928** Radclyffe Hall's *The Well of Loneliness* is published.

**1933** Adolf Hitler comes to power in Germany; begins persecution of homosexuals.

Magnus Hirschfeld's work and research is destroyed.

**1941** The United States enters World War II.

**1943** Jim Kepner begins what becomes known as ONE National Gay and Lesbian Archive.

**1945** The first organization for gay veterans, the Veterans' Benevolent Association, is founded.

**1948** Alfred Kinsey publishes *Sexual Behavior in the Human Male.*

**1951** The Mattachine Society is founded in Los Angeles, California.

Christine Jorgensen completes her gender affirmation surgery in Denmark.

**1952** The American Psychiatric Association publishes the first edition of the *Diagnostic and Statistical Manual,* which classifies homosexuality as a sociopathic personality disorder.

**1953** Alfred Kinsey publishes *Sexual Behavior in the Human Female.*

**1955** The first lesbian activist group, the Daughters of Bilitis, is founded in San Francisco, California.

**1961** José Sarria becomes the first openly gay candidate for public office in the United States.

**1966** A police raid on Compton's Cafeteria in San Francisco turns into a riot, marking the birth of the transgender liberation movement.

**1969** A police raid on the Stonewall Inn in New York City becomes a riot when gay, lesbian, bisexual, and transgender people resist police harassment.

**1970** The first gay pride celebration takes place on the first anniversary of Christopher Street Liberation Day.

# GLOSSARY

**bisexual** Having attraction to both sexes.

**blacklist** To prohibit someone from working somewhere because of ideology or identity.

**blue discharge** A type of neutral military discharge that was often used to remove homosexuals from military service.

**cisgender** Describing a person whose gender matches their biological sex.

**Cold War** A decades-long period of tension following World War II between the communist Soviet Union and the United States. It was marked by each superpower's attempt to influence or force other countries to commit to its ideological political identity and become military allies.

**cross-dress** To wear clothes, makeup, and accessories that the opposite sex usually wears (e.g. a cisgender man wearing women's clothing and makeup).

**cruising** Looking for sexual partners in public.

**drag** A performance in which men or women cross-dress and sing or act in some way that is typical of the gender they are depicting.

**gay** An informal term that means homosexual. It is typical for both sexes to use this term when describing their sexuality.

**gender identity** A person's internal sense of gender, often expressed through behavior, clothing, hairstyle, voice, or body characteristics. An individual's gender identity is completely unrelated to any aspect of that person's anatomy or sexual attraction to others.

**Hays Code** The limitations on the content a movie could contain that was used between 1930 and the late 1960s.

**homophile** Relating to homosexuals and or homosexuality in a positive way.

**homosexual** A person who is attracted exclusively to people of the same sex.

**lavender scare** A panic in the 1950s that led the US government to fire or otherwise remove many accused and actual gay men and lesbians and other queers from government jobs.

**lesbian** A term used exclusively to describe a female homosexual.

**outed** When a person's LGBTQ+ status has been exposed either intentionally or accidentally.

**passing** Presenting oneself as part of a social group that the person doesn't belong to, like a gay woman pretending to be straight.

**pseudonym** A name someone uses in place of their legal name.

**red scare** A 1950s panic in which people were removed from government jobs because of suspected communist ties or beliefs.

**sexology** The scientific study of human sexuality.

**sexual orientation** Describes the inclination of an individual in terms of their sexual attraction toward others or sexual behaviors. Sexual orientation and gender identity are completely unrelated.

**sodomy**  A legal term used to describe gay sex or sex that cannot produce offspring.

**speakeasy**  A secret illegal bar from the era of Prohibition.

**transgender**  Identifying with a gender that is different from the one assigned at birth.

# FOR MORE INFORMATION

The Ali Forney Center (AFC)
321 West 125th Street
New York, NY 10027
(212) 206-0574
Website: http://www.aliforneycenter.org
Facebook: @AliForney
Twitter: @AliForneyCenter
The AFC is the largest organization in the United
    States dedicated to providing resources,
    including housing, job preparedness, and
    health care services, for LGBTQ+ youth who
    are homeless.

Canadian Lesbian and Gay Archives
34 Isabella Street
Toronto, ON M4Y 1N1
Canada
(416) 777-2755
Website: http://www.clga.ca
Facebook: @CLGArchives
Twitter: @clgarchives
This organization has the largest independent
    LGBTQ+ archive in the world and emphasizes
    Canadian LGBTQ+ history.

Gerber/Hart Library and Archives
6500 N Clark Street
Chicago, IL 60626
(773) 381-8030
Website: http://www.gerberhart.org
Facebook: @GerberHart

Twitter and Instagram: @gerberhart
This organization features an extensive collection
of books and periodicals. It also hosts
events, including book discussion groups, film
screenings, and game nights.

GLBT Historical Society Archives and Museum
4127 18th Street
San Francisco, CA 94114
(415) 621-1107
Website: http://www.glbthistory.org
Facebook: @GLBTHistory
Youtube: @glbthistory
Considered a leader in the field of public LGBTQ+
history, this San Francisco–based society
preserves history and hosts community events.

Lesbian, Gay, Bisexual, & Transgender Community
Center
208 West 13th Street
New York, NY 10011
(212) 620-7310
Website: https://gaycenter.org
Facebook: @lgbtcenternyc
Twitter: @LGBTCenterNYC
This organization features community spaces, a
bookstore, and a coffee shop.

ONE Archives at the University of Southern California
909 West Adams Boulevard
Los Angeles, CA 90007
(213) 821-2771
Website: http://one.usc.edu

Facebook: @onearchives

Twitter and YouTube: @ONEarchives

These archives offer an international collection of LGBTQ+ artifacts that is open to the public. This organization also features exhibitions of historical materials.

Rainbow Health Ontario

Sherbourne Health Centre

333 Sherbourne Street

Toronto, ON M5A 2S5

Canada

(416) 324-4100

Website: http://www.rainbowhealthontario.ca

Facebook: @RainbowHealthOntario

Twitter: @RainbowHealthOn

YouTube: @Rainbow Health Ontario

This Ontario-based initiative advocates for LGBTQ+ health and provides resources for groups with a similar aim.

# FOR FURTHER READING

Arora, Sabina G. *The Great Migration and the Harlem Renaissance.* (African American Experience: From Slavery to the Presidency). New York, NY: Rosen Publishing, 2016.

Barker, Meg-John. *Queer: A Graphic History.* London, UK: Icon Books, 2016

Bausum, Ann. *Stonewall: Breaking Out in the Fight for Gay Rights.* New York, NY: Penguin Random House, 2015.

Beemyn, Genny. *A Queer Capital: A History of Gay Life in Washington, D.C.* New York, NY: Routledge, 2015.

Brooks, Adrian. *The Right Side of History: 100 Years of LGBTQI Activism.* New York, NY: Cleis Press, 2015.

Deschamps, David. *LGBTQ Stats.* New York, NY: New Press, 2017.

Henneberg, Susan. *James Baldwin: Groundbreaking Author and Civil Rights Activist.* New York, NY: Rosen Publishing, 2015.

Llanas, Sheila Griffin. *Walt Whitman* (Great American Authors). Minneapolis, MN: ABDO, 2013.

Morlock, Theresa. *LGBTQ Human Rights Movement: Civic Participation Working for Human Rights.* New York, NY: Rosen Publishing, 2017.

Poehlmann, Tristan. *The Stonewall Riots: The Fight for LGBT Rights.* Minneapolis, MN: Essential Library, 2017.

Pohlen, Jerome. *Gay & Lesbian History for Kids: The Century-Long Struggle for LGBT Rights, with 21 Activities*. Chicago, IL: Chicago Review Press, 2016.

Ristock, Janice L. *Intimate Partner Violence in LGBTQ Lives*. New York, NY: Routledge, 2013.

Springate, Megan E. *LGBTQ America: A Theme Study of Lesbian, Gay, Bisexual, Transgender, and Queer History*. Washington, DC: National Park Foundation, 2016.

Stewart, Dafina Lazarus, Kristen A. Renn, and G. Blue Brazelton. *Gender and Sexual Diversity in U.S. Higher Education: Contexts and Opportunities for LGBTQ College Students*. San Francisco, CA: Jossey-Bass, 2015.

# BIBLIOGRAPHY

Adam, Barry D. *The Rise of a Gay and Lesbian Movement*. Boston, MA: G. K. Hall & Co, 1987.

Amani, Cairo. "Queer Harlem: From LGBT Icons of the Harlem Renaissance to Invisible Me." Autostraddle, April 4, 2012. https://www .autostraddle.com/queer-harlem-from-lgbt-icons -of-the-harlem-renaissance-to-invisible-me -135971.

Atkins, Gary L. *Gay Seattle: Stories of Exile and Belonging*. Seattle, WA: University of Washington Press, 2003.

Baim, Tracy. *Out and Proud in Chicago*. Evanston, IL: Surrey Books, 2008.

Baim, Tracy, and John D'Emilio. *Gay Press, Gay Power: The Growth of LGBT Community Newspapers in America*. Chicago, IL: Prairie Avenue Productions and Windy City Media, 2012.

Bausum, Ann. *Stonewall: Breaking Out in the Fight for Gay Rights*. New York, NY: Penguin Random House, 2015.

Beard, Rick, and Leslie Cohn Berlowitz. *Greenwich Village: Culture and Counterculture*. New York, NY: Museum of the City of New York, 1993.

Berube, Allen. *Coming Out Under Fire: The History of Gay Men and Women in World War II*. Chapel Hill, NC: University of North Carolina Press, 1990.

Bronski, Michael. *A Queer History of the United States*. Boston, MA: Beacon Press, 2011.

Brooks, Adrian. *The Right Side of History: 100 Years of LGBTQI Activism*. New York, NY: Cleis Press, 2015.

Boyd, Nan Alamilla. *Wide Open Town: A Queer History of San Francisco*. Berkeley, CA: University of California Press, 2003.

Eaklor, Vicki L. *Queer America: A GLBT History of the 20th Century*. Westport, CT: Greenwood Press, 2008.

Eisner, Shiri. *Bi: Notes for a Bisexual Revolution*. Berkeley, CA: Seal Press, 2013.

Hogan, Steve, and Lee Hudson. *Completely Queer: The Gay and Lesbian Encyclopedia*. New York, NY: Henry Holt and Company, 1999.

Katz, Jonathan Ned. *Gay American History: Lesbians and Gay Men in the USA*. New York, NY: Meridian, 1992.

Kuhn, Betsy. *Gay Power! The Stonewall Riots and the Gay Rights Movement*. Minneapolis, MN: Twenty-First Century Books, 2011.

Stewart, William, Emily Hamer, and Frances Williams. *Cassell's Queer Companion: A Dictionary of Lesbian and Gay Life and Culture*. London, UK: Cassell, 1995.

Streitmatter, Rodger. *Outlaw Marriages: The Hidden Histories of Fifteen Extraordinary Same-Sex Couples*. Boston, MA: Beacon Press, 2012.

Villarosa, Linda. *The Gay Harlem Renaissance*. The Root, July 23, 2011. http://www.theroot.com/the-gay-harlem-renaissance-1790864926.

Weiss, Jillian T. "GL vs. BT: The Archaeology of Biphobia and Transphobia within the U.S. Gay and Lesbian Community." *Journal of Bisexuality*, Vol. 3 (January 15, 2004): 25–55. https://ssrn.com/abstract=1649428.

# INDEX

# ABOUT THE AUTHOR

Greg Baldino holds a bachelor of arts degree in fiction writing from Columbia College Chicago, where he studied literature and twentieth-century cultural history. Since 2007, he has written as a journalist and essayist on topics such as alternative fashion, folk music, Italian cooking, criminal psychology, antifascist activism, digital media, comics and graphic novels, gender politics, environmental science, and the performing arts. He was born on the anniversary of the Stonewall riots and according to his coffee mug is the World's Okayest Bisexual.

# PHOTO CREDITS